You Might As Well

by

Segun Olowookere

ISBN: 978-1-326-78934-3

PublishNation
www.publishnation.co.uk

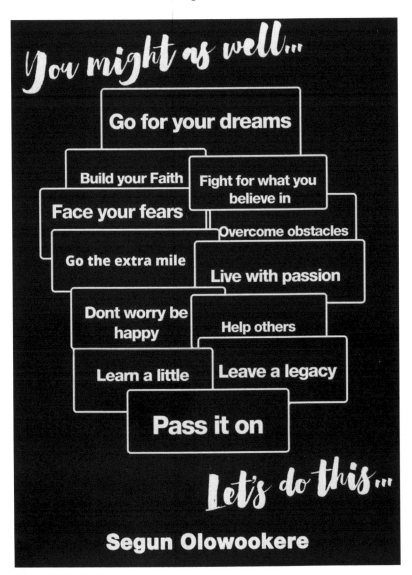

"Success in life starts from the mindset. Our abilities to feel happy and fulfilled begin with us imagining first what that life would look like. This book is a great start to that process as it arms you with all the tools to exercise your mind - that special muscle, as well as providing some strong examples of how prominent figures have achieved success through correct thinking. Well worth a read."

Augusta Onyiuke-Eluma
Property Finance Specialist
Financial Planning for you, your family and your business

"In a confused and uncertain world Segun has written the book 'You Might as Well' at a perfect time. The book is like a breath of fresh air full of motivation and insights that anyone can learn and implement in their everyday lives. Read the book and then pass it on."

Bode Olowookere
Property Entrepreneur, author of the book 'Make the shift to Success' Investor, Consultant & Speaker

I dedicate this book to my beautiful wife and my son. You are both very special and amazing.

Thank you Lord. I love my life. ☺

Thank you Tracy for staying on me to finish this book and then reading it and giving me your honest feedback. Jessica, Liz, Bode, Gus and Jenny, thank you for your advice, time, and feedback. You are amazing...

When you have family you are super lucky so I want to say thank you to my family. Mum, Dad, Aramide, Seyi, Bode, Ade and all of my nieces and nephews. I did this for you too. To my super amazing foster mum you planted the seeds from day one. I am forever grateful.

I have had many life teachers and mentors. To you all I say thank you.

Michael Hastings you are my hero and I am forever grateful for your love and support.

Much love.
Segun

Foreword

It's always said that the best things are free...
and most jump to good health and generous love
and having breath and the rising of the sun as
the proof points – and they are!

But in this book of nuggets we discover a
catalogue of other gems – none commercially
obtainable and with no currency price tag. These
free gifts carry a cost but not a price.

Here, in these uplifting pages Segun has elevated
the artful phrases passed around between the
philosophical and made us pause – made me stop
hard and fast and ask:

> ➢   Am I on track to secure my legacy?

> ➢   Have I given enough passion to drive
> transformation rather than just
> change?

> ➢   Am I curious and learning every day in a
> way that ends indulgence and shifts my

4

focus to how to achieve and not just to plan?

> Are my dreams, my faith and my determination in line for that which must come on not just after me but through me ...?

These questions, which this tablet of wisdom contains, find answers in real vivid men and women of history – like Mary Seacole, Rosa Parks, Bob Marley or even Mohammed Ali ....and so many others. I learnt so so much. I genuinely gained insights that I thought I was well worn in...but not till this city of truth hit me again and I saw it.

We must energise ourselves for the fight of purpose not the flight of pleasure. Our world shouts 'you deserve the best – go rest '– our purpose calls gently 'you give the best and the rest will refresh you '

I have to say this – don't put it down. Finish it in one go. Then stand up, face the mirror and pledge. Then go again – chapter by chapter – one a day. If you do, like me, you will renew all you thought you knew and this time, the hero will be you.

Michael Hastings
Lord Dr HASTINGS of Scarisbrick CBE
Vice President of UNICEF
Trustee, Vodafone Foundation
President ZANE (Zimbabwe)
Global Head of Citizenship - KPMG International
Independent Peer, House of Lords

Introduction

I decided to write this book to share my experiences and some of the things I have learnt so far in my life journey. I have been studying some of the most impactful leaders of the last century. I am privileged to be exposed to these principles and there is no better time than now to share these with YOU.

To help us master things in life it is good to get some motivational reminders that inspire us to take action. I have written this book for everyone who sometimes feels like they are experiencing a bad day, week, month, year or even a bad life!

It is important that we all stay strong and help each other. Your will and desire to take the time to read this book gave me the motivation to write it. I am confident that you will be empowered and challenged by this book to take action and pass it on to someone else.

- ✓ If you feel that you are not good, enough or that things are just not happening for you. This book is for you.

- ✓ If you feel alone, low in confidence, misled, misguided and with no direction. This book is for you.

- ✓ If you feel comfortable with life and are doing ok but believe deep down that there is more to life. This book is also for you.

This is a book full of positive energy, practical motivation, inspiration and encouragement. Together we can make it happen.

The book is broken into 12 short chapters and is easy to read. If you would not normally read a book, try this book because just like you I never used to like reading. I read my first book at the age of 21.

My goal is for you to be inspired and empowered to take more action towards your dream and maybe even read some more books...you might as well...let's do this...

Contents

1) Go for your dreams
2) Build your faith
3) Fight for what you believe in
4) Face your fears
5) Overcome obstacles
6) Go the extra mile
7) Live with passion
8) Don't worry, be happy
9) Help others
10) Learn a little
11) Leave a legacy
12) Pass it on

MOTIVATION, INSPIRATION, WORDS OF WISDOM, HISTORY, PICTURES, and PRACTICAL ACTION TIPS all in one simple to read book written by Segun Olowookere especially for YOU!

Go for your dreams

A dream is something you greatly desire.
Dreams are available to everyone and they are
traded for your thoughts and time. All it
takes is for you to close your eyes and imagine
that you are in a place where you want to be,
in possession of something that you want to
have or become the person that you aspire to
be and a dream has been created.

11

Your dreams take you past your reality. Your dream(s) give you energy. They inspire you. The bigger your dream the more action you will be inspired to take.

Dreams start in our heart. Our minds talk us out of our dream. The challenges of life, our logical thoughts, the media and sometimes even our friends and family persuade us to settle for less than our dreams.

We all begin our life with a dream. Somewhere down the line, some of us stop dreaming. Keep dreaming and go for your dreams...it is possible!

If you could wake up tomorrow and have the life, you truly want. What would it look like?

The story of Dr Martin Luther King Jr is probably the most famous dream in modern history.

On 28th August 1963 Dr Martin Luther King Jr (Dr King) delivered his *I have a dream* speech in front of 200,000 people. During this speech, he called for racial equality and an end to discrimination.

Dr King also addressed the economic and unemployment problems of all disadvantaged people. We will all have an opinion on whether this dream has become a reality since, but one thing for sure is that this was a big dream and Dr Martin Luther King Jr dedicated his life towards achieving this dream.

Sometimes our dream (such as Dr Martin Luther King's) will be so big that we will need to dedicate our lives to it.

My dream is to be the best family man I can be, the best husband, father, son and brother. My dream is to become the greatest motivational finance trainer in the world and help people understand money, motivation and purpose. My dream is to help increase the consciousness of the next generation. This will help bring more positive energy, more togetherness, unity, belief and the financial resources to fund the journey towards everyone's dream(s).

Everyday life can sometimes take our dreams away from us. Don't let everyday life take your dreams away. Keep believing and keep fighting for your dream(s).

> *3 top tips to help you go for your dreams:*
>
> 1. *Write your dreams down*
> 2. *Read your dreams regularly and picture yourself experiencing your dreams*
> 3. *Take action towards your dreams every day. No matter what*

It is very important to have faith in yourself. It is your responsibility to take action towards your dreams. Once you have confidence and faith in yourself, no one can take your dreams away from you.

- Dream your dreams
- Make the decision to go for your dreams
- Dreams can and do come true
- Help others dreams come true and yours will do too

In the words of Dr Martin Luther King Jr
"I have a dream today"

Be all you can be, find your dreams. Don't give up or talk yourself out of your dreams. Have faith in yourself...believe in your dreams...faith demands action...no one can take your dreams away from you...what is this dream that you have?

YOU might as well...GO FOR YOUR DREAMS...Let's do this!

15

Build your faith

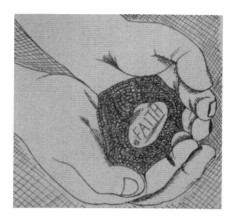

Faith is having complete trust or confidence in someone or something. Faith is belief beyond your abilities, skills, control and decisions. Faith is so real that you can prove it through the strength of your belief. Faith starts at the point of our human limitation. Faith makes you move from where you are now to where you want to be.

Faith is visualising and believing in the achievement of a dream. There are no limits to the mind except those that we acknowledge. Faith goes beyond our thoughts. It becomes part of our DNA.

Faith helps us get through the journey of life. Everyday our faith is called upon us. You might as well begin to build your faith now because you are going to need it to help you survive today and thrive tomorrow.

We all have some kind of faith. The simplest of all faiths is what we could call natural faith. An example of natural faith is the faith that you had when you went to go and sit on the chair that you are currently sitting on. You did not check to make sure that it was strong enough to hold your weight. You just sat down believing that it would hold your weight.

Imagine that you had this level of belief in everything you did. No doubt, no procrastination, no second-guessing, no what if's. Only action with full confidence in achieving the goal or the dream. If you could move towards something with this level of belief, what would you do?

Sometimes we put our faith in other people, systems or institutions such as our family, our employers, or our banks. Again, these are examples of where we use our faith every day.

Faith is the substance of things hoped for, the evidence of things not seen. The more we want to grow, do and become the more we need our faith. How do we do something we have never done before? How do we overcome challenges and problems that seem bigger than us? It takes faith. It takes an inner fire that was lit before or during the challenge. Awaken that powerful, fearless lion inside of you.

Eric Thomas was born in Detroit, Michigan, USA and was raised by his mother and his father who

he later found out (in his teenage years) was not
his real father.

Whilst growing up there were times when Eric
received beatings from his step father and this
led him to take the decision to leave home and he
blamed his mother for not protecting him.

Eric was 16 years old and homeless in Detroit
where the temperature drops below zero. He
spent many nights sleeping in abandoned buildings
and fed himself by looking for food in bins. This
lifestyle led Eric to drop out of high school
before completing his final exams.

During this time, Detroit was well known for gang
related activity. Eric did not choose to follow the
gangster lifestyle, which could have been the
easy option at this time of his life.

Eric's life changed when someone told him that
they saw greatness in him. He was still homeless
in Detroit but he started to dream and build his
faith. He found a new set of life principles
through the church and started living his life
with the Ten Commandments close to his heart.

Soon after Eric's wife (then girlfriend) went to college (university) and asked Eric to follow her and complete college.

Eric followed his wife to college and fought hard to complete his final high school exams. He did and went on to graduate from college. It took him 12 years but he eventually completed his 4-year college degree facing many obstacles and challenges along the way. During this time, Eric also set up community projects helping young people such as young single mothers and young men involved in the gangster lifestyle pass their high school exams.

He set these projects up with very little money, no sponsorship or government grant. Even though these projects were having a great impact, he received very little support from the local community and almost had to stop running the programme but he managed to keep it going.

Today Dr Eric Thomas is happily married with two children. He travels the world motivating and inspiring professional sports teams, companies and individuals. The amazing thing is how he started to become the best empowerment speaker in the world.

It all started with Eric, quitting his secure job with a wife, two kids and home to pay for. He created motivational videos (TGIM – Thank God it's Monday) and put these videos on YouTube. He then began speaking at schools and pursued his dream.

Things did not just happen overnight for Dr Eric Thomas. He needed faith to see his vision and go for it. I am not saying that you need to quit your job and go for it, as there was also lots of hard work, learning and skill involved, which are also very important. However, without the step of faith it would have remained a dream and not become a reality for Eric.

Another amazing thing is that at the time of writing this book Eric will tell you that his ultimate goal is to win a Nobel peace prize for inspiring humanity. So he is still dreaming. Not only that, it also took the trust and faith from his wife to support Eric when taking that step.

Faith is one of the most powerful emotions, alongside love and sex. It is a state of being that needs to be developed constantly.

3 top tips to help develop your faith?

1) *Increase your knowledge in the area we want to grow in. Increased knowledge and skill helps increase faith*
2) *Learn to control your mind when doubt and negative thoughts come by using meditation and positive words*
3) *Listen and read the positive words again and again to ingrain it in your mind*

Faith can also be linked to trust and it can take time to develop the level of trust that allows us to operate at a higher level.

You know when your faith has grown, as you feel more empowered. This means that you have been enlightened and have the energy, information and confidence to move on, even though there is no clear path in front of you.

- Your level of faith is positively correlated to the strength of the character inside of you.
- Faith is a state of mind, which you may develop at will.
- Faith is the starting point of all achievements.
- Faith is trusting in a higher power and energy beyond our human capacity.
- Lack of faith is doubt.

There are times when motivation and encouragement (such as reading this book) will not work and you will need to call upon a power greater than yourself!

'Whatever your natural reaction would be, when faith comes you go in the opposite direction.' Bishop TD Jakes.

Norman Vincent Peale said, "What seems impossible one minute becomes, through faith, possible the next".

Science says show me and I will believe. Faith says believe and I will show you.

I like to describe taking a step of faith like this. Imagine that you are in a corridor that is pitch Black. You cannot see a thing. You have two choices. Walk along the corridor or turn around and open the door behind you, which you know is unlocked. Choosing to walk along the corridor is taking that step of faith believing that there will be light as you walk and an unlocked door at the end of the corridor.

Believe that there is something special and powerful inside of you. Build your faith. Just as people spend time working out building their muscles or building a team. We need to build our faith. Faith does not work unless we do. With faith, all things are possible; it is up to you to believe it.

YOU might as well...BUILD YOUR FAITH...Let's do this!

Fight for what you believe in

The word *fight* does not always refer to two people beating each other to the ground, blow after blow. There is another definition of the word that can be described as; 'striving to obtain or accomplish something' even though there maybe challenges and obstacles in the way.

People will always try to influence our thinking and our beliefs but it is our individual responsibility to take the time to discover what we believe is true for ourselves.

Before you start fighting for something make, sure that it is in your heart and it is something or someone that you truly believe in.

26

The inner fight is a conflict of values, where your actions do not match your inner values and principles. Have you ever been in a position where you had to do something that went against your values? How did this make you feel?

I remember growing up as a teenager and being forced through peer pressure to take on certain beliefs that went against my core values. I felt like I was selling myself out and living a lie to keep others happy and smoking a whole load of weed to help numb the pain.

I have always had big dreams for my life and a passion to help make the world a more joyful place for those who have difficult lives. I believed that by the time I hit 25 my life will be taking great shape with some of my dreams already done and dusted. I turned 25 and I realized that my lifestyle was not helping me move towards my dreams. I had to make a choice. Fight for my lifestyle or fight my dreams.

This describes the inner fight. The inner fight occurs in your mind, heart and soul. Your mind goes to work trying to make sense of it all but your heart and soul do not allow your mind to accept it as being OK. This fight separates the men and women from the boys and girls when the time comes to stand up and be counted.

Rosa Louise McCauley Parks was an African-American civil rights activist. After working all day, Rosa boarded the Cleveland Avenue bus at around 6 p.m. on Thursday, 1 December 1955, in the city of Montgomery, USA. She paid her fare and sat in an empty seat in the first row of back seats that had been reserved for Black people only, in the 'colored' section of the bus. It was near the middle of the bus and directly behind

the front seats of the bus, which had been specifically reserved for White passengers.
As the bus traveled along its regular route, all of the *'White-only'* seats in the bus started to fill up. The bus reached the third stop and several white passengers boarded. Following protocol, the bus driver noted that the front seats of the bus were full with White passengers and there were now two or three White passengers standing. He moved the 'colored' section sign back a few rows behind Rosa Parks and demanded that four Black people (including Rosa) give up their seats in the middle section so that the White passengers could sit down.

Rosa Parks refused to obey the bus driver's order that she give up her seat to make room for a White passenger. The bus driver ended up having to call the police and had Rosa Park's arrested.

This incident changed the life of Rosa Parks and she became an iconic figure for *standing up for what you believe in.* She was not the first Black women to not give up her seat, for a White passenger but she ended up dedicating her life to her belief and took the fight to the highest possible level.

I am sure that many of us can think of a time when we have put in a lot of effort to stick up for someone or something that we feel is important to us. Think, why you did this? How did you feel afterwards?

Every day we are faced with situations where we can impose our stand on our beliefs and values. These beliefs and values can be as simple as smiling and saying good morning to a passerby or allowing an elderly person to sit down on the train out of respect.

Being an older brother, I can remember many times when I have stepped in to protect my siblings from trouble even though it meant putting myself at risk of being disciplined. The fight is choosing the right action in the moment to help us apply our values and principles through our journey of life.

3 top tips to help you fight for what you believe in:

1. Follow your heart and values
2. Be strong in the moment
3. Fight with intelligence and stay committed to your values

Fighting for what we believe in is not just fighting and arguing any time, we feel like it. Sometimes the fight may require silence and no action as our feelings may be telling us to do something that goes against our values and principles. The real fight is learning to knock out the wrong feeling and make the right decision in the moment.

Before you can fight for what you believe in you need to have a strong understanding of your values and principles. They need to be personal to you. This does not mean that other people will not have the same or similar values and principles as you but it will mean that you will have a strong personal understanding of these values and principles for yourself.

At the same time, respect other people's opinions but protect your values, principles, and others who are vulnerable. That's one of my values.

Rosa Parks said some years later after the event that had occurred on the bus that many people had said that she refused to get up because she was tired after a hard day's work. She agreed to part of this. She said that she was tired, not physically tired after a day's work but tired of giving in.

Many people say that they will fight for their friends, family and loved ones. Some people make the sacrifice to fight for their country. Some people fight against the policy makers. If there is something in your heart or life that you love or something that makes you angry, cry or fills you with passion, fight for it!

+ Fight for what you believe in
+ Stand up and be counted
+ Fight hard
+ Fight fair
+ Be strong

+ Be determined
+ Have courage
+ Are you fighting to live or living to fight?

An old African proverb says; 'If you don't stand for something then you will fall for something'. Therefore, I ask you. What are you standing for?

> Dr Martin Luther King Jr said, "Our lives begin to end the moment we stay silent about the things that matter".

Let's stop fighting our inner thoughts and feelings and start fighting the real fights. These fights will make a positive change in our lives and the lives of others.

Have values and principles. Be unique, respect other people's opinions but make your own life decisions. Protect your values and principles as well as the values and principles of others who are vulnerable.

YOU might as well...FIGHT FOR WHAT YOU BELIEVE IN...Let's do this!

Face your fears

Fear stands for 'false evidence appearing real'. It is an illusion. How and why do we show fear about something that has not yet happened? We should only ever have fear in the moment.

Fear causes paralysis. Fear isolates you and keeps you locked up in your own world. Fear limits and restricts you. Fear and insecurity are best friends and much of it is imagined. It uses our imagination in a negative way. When this occurs, we need to turn it around and learn to use our imagination in a positive way. Focus our minds on something good that can come out of the situation or circumstance.

I started writing this book in 2012. After writing the first draft, I put it down and did not work on it again for years. The real reason for this was not that I did not have the time but was scared. Scared of completing the book because I knew that I would need to put it out there and receive feedback from people as well as expose some of my life experiences and inner thoughts.

A lot of time and energy is wasted having fear for something that has not yet or even going to happen. Fear is an unreal emotion that our minds create to keep us safe. To make the most of life, we must face our fears and move through them.

I finished my book because I knew deep down that I could help someone by sharing my thoughts and learning's from life so far. I just had to overcome the fear of exposing my inner thoughts and receiving feedback on them. It was holding me back. It was me being selfish as I believe me sharing my experiences and learning's in this book are helping others today.

It has been scientifically proven that humans are born with two fears only;

1) The fear of falling
2) The fear of loud noises.

This means that all other fears that exist, were picked up from the environment around you. Things you have seen heard and experienced. The same way that you have learnt the fear means that it is possible to unlearn the fear and take it out of your belief system. The best way to do this is to confront your fears bit-by-bit, inch by inch and step by step. Build up your resilience towards the fear. Sometimes however we need to take a big step and jump in with everything relying on our faith to pull us through.

Fear of the unknown is very common and this can often lead to procrastination. Don't stop and wait, keep going forward. When you stop, you lose the momentum. I was once told 'it is harder to push start a car that is stationary compared to a car that is rolling at 1mph'. Don't let fear slow you down or even try to stop you. Time is ticking and the door of opportunity will not stay open forever.

After working as finance assistant for an international think tank for 3 years I became bored and wanted to learn more and progress my career. It was quite a small organization and I knew that I would not be able to get a promotion as we were only a small finance team of three and my manager was not going anywhere.

I was very comfortable and had built up some great working relationships with my manager and others in the wider team. In this moment I knew that I had to leave but I was scared as I did, not

*have another job lined up and did not have
enough savings to keep me going for more than a
month. I felt the fear and resigned. In the end,
it all worked out great and the decision took me
to an amazing organization that enabled me to
grow, learn, meet new people and exposed me to
my passion for travel and training.*

When fear creeps in think about the risks
involved and plan for the potential risks. Once
you have done this, take action! There will always
be some level of uncertainty but that is what
keeps us alive. What do you have to lose? What
is the worst that can happen? Imagine knowing
the outcome of your every move for the rest of
your life. There would be no point in living
because you would already know what is going to
happen.

Fear of being wrong only slows you down. It
keeps you in a sleeper hold. Don't be afraid to try
something. If it doesn't work out then learn from
it. At least you will have a sense of peace knowing
that you gave it a shot. However, don't stop
there! Go again; using your previous experience,

knowledge, and courage. You know what they say, 'whatever doesn't kill you only makes you stronger'. Have faith; face your fears and grow in strength.

> *3 top tips to help you overcome fear;*
>
> 1) *Embrace the fear*
> 2) *Face the fear*
> 3) *Keep moving because the fear will come right back if you stop*

I once heard a wise man say.

'If you are not prepared to face your fears
You cannot grow
If you cannot grow
Then you cannot be your best
If you cannot be your best then you cannot be happier
If you cannot be happier then what else is there!'

In order to go for our dreams we need to have faith and overcome our fears along the way. The first thing to note is that fear never just goes away if you do not make the decision to overcome it. Every time you want to move to a new level there will be some kind of fear. This is good as it keeps you alive. It means that you are about to grow.

Fella Kuti the African musician and activist said at the start of one of his songs, 'the secret to life is to have no fear'.

Feel the fear and do it anyway. You can move a little bit at a time or you can jump right in! The most influential people are the bravest people. Remember that fear stands for **false evidence appearing real**. What is the worst that can happen?

YOU might as well...FACE YOUR FEARS...Let's do this!

Overcome obstacles

Even once, we pluck up the belief, faith, passion, courage, positive mindset and energy to face our fears we are likely to face barriers and may even hit a wall. This is painful, very de-motivating and sometimes it feels like we are moving backwards because of all the challenges and obstacles that try to slow us down and hinder our progress.

Have you heard of the saying 'It feels like you are going two steps forwards and three steps backwards'? This is not the case. Even though you may not feel like you are moving forward in the physical, you are still moving.

You are strengthening your inner self just as the roots of a tree grow downward first, out of sight. A skyscraper is started by digging a deep hole in the ground. The obstacles that come your way will allow you to stand tall and strong sooner or later as long as you keep fighting.

Failure cannot cope with persistence. Keep going. Do not let the obstacles stop you. If you can't get over it, then go under it. If you can't get under it then go around it and if you can't go around it then take a step backwards, ask for some help and charge your way through it! The door will open. Some doors are locked by time but your endless will, determination and, desire is the key.

Another word for an obstacle could be a problem. Be a problem solver not a whiner. It would be almost impossible to climb a smooth mountain.

Les Brown one the greatest motivational speakers in the world says that; 'If life knocks you down then try to land on your back because if you can look up, you can GET UP!'

As humans, we have been solving problems and overcoming obstacles since our creation. Obstacles help make us smarter, stronger and help take us to the next level.

One of my biggest life obstacles was when I moved out of my parents' house for the second time, at the age of 20. I had just landed an internship position after 7 months of searching and countless rejections. Four weeks later, I found myself in a hospital bed with a drip attached to my arm supplying my body fluids as I had been diagnosed with Tuberculosis (TB). This absolutely knocked me for six, my body was dying and my pride was diminished. After 5 nights in the hospital, I was discharged and I had to move back to my parent's house.

I am now thankful that they accepted me back after leaving for the second time. This was the most painful and largest obstacle I had to overcome. I could not continue my internship and felt like I had gone backwards in life. It took all of my faith and determination to fight through the illness, re-build my body and get my mind to a level of sanity and peace.

Just like a pilot asks passengers to fasten their seat belt on take-off, know that every time you plan to move forward you will need to fasten your seatbelt because the journey ahead will have obstacles. The good news is that all of the obstacles will make you stronger and prepare you for your new destination.

Just like a plan, life is a journey that takes you where you choose to go. There will be challenges along the way but the power behind you is greater than the challenge in front of you.

Look at obstacles like a training exercise.
Understand that the challenge will make you
stronger and help you along the journey of life.
Not all things feel good but they can still work
for the good. Some obstacles will help you find
your passion, some will help you discover new
skills, and abilities, which you did not know you,
had inside of you.

Whilst recovering from TB I read my first book.
It was a book on black history and this really
helped me learn and understand who I was which
was critical in me overcoming the challenge of
starting life again at the age of 20 when all of
my friends were living life to the full. I
discovered my passion for Africa and had a
burning desire to learn more about the history of
the world and Africa. Reading is something I now
do every day without fail and I am constantly
reading positive words to encourage me and help
build my faith.

When you face a challenge or a life obstacle, find
the right information and people to help you get
through. My information came from books and my

people were my family. During these challenges keep your mind and eyes open to the epiphany that may also come your way during this time like my love for reading and Africa.

Everyone wants to be happy and nobody wants to feel pain but you can't make rainbows without rain. Rain aids the growth process. Just as rain helps flowers grow, obstacles help us blossom.

Maya Angelou was an award winning poet and writer who had to overcome some massive obstacles during her early years. Maya's name at birth was Marguerite Annie Johnson.

Her parents split up when she was very young and she and her brother went to live with her father's mother. Her grandmother lived in Arkansas, USA. Whilst staying here Maya faced lots of racial abuse.

At the age of seven, her mother's boyfriend raped Maya. When her uncle heard about this, he killed the man. These experiences forced Maya to shut down and she stopped talking.

During World War II Maya moved to San Francisco, California and won a scholarship to study dance and acting. At the age of 16, she got pregnant, had a son, and ended up having to work several jobs to support herself and her baby.

It was not until the mid 1950s that Maya started to gain some success in her career as a musical performer and singer. Maya was also a strong civil rights activist and worked closely with the Southern Christian Leadership Conference (SCLC) where Dr King was the leader. Dr King and Maya were very good friends and he was actually assassinated on Maya's birthday on April 4 1968. This caused her to stop celebrating her birthday for many years.

In the 60s, Maya lived overseas, later returned to the USA, and wrote 'I Know Why the Caged Bird Sings'. This memoir was based on her life experiences and it turned Maya into an international star.

The message from just a few of many challenges and obstacles that Maya Angelou faced during her life is a testimony of what we can achieve if we do not let obstacles stop us or get in the way of our dreams.

Sometimes it is the things in the past that become our biggest obstacles. These obstacles are often emotional, spiritual and can normally be traced to our childhood experiences. Deal with it all now so that it does not come back to haunt you later. Just like fear, obstacles from the past do not just go away. We need to make a decision to deal with it.

One of the biggest obstacles that slow people down is themselves. Stop dwelling on the past. Forgive and focus ahead. If you choose not to forgive then you are just carrying another burden around your neck. We all make mistakes especially towards those closest to us.

One amazing example of someone being hurt and using that experience to help them become a better person was Adele. Adele is an English singer and songwriter who broke up with her boyfriend and then found out that he was engaged to be married only a few months later. This must have been very upsetting and almost unforgivable but Adele decided to write a song about it (Someone like You) and that song went on to become a number 1 hit and sell over 10 million copies around the world and still counting.

Do not let resentment keep you bogged down. Life will throw enough challenges your way as it is, so focus ahead on your goals and dreams. Holding onto things of the past is like trying to run with weights on. Think of how much more energy you will have and how much quicker you will arrive at your destination if you chose to drop those weights and burdens.

3 top tips to help you overcome obstacles;

1) *Stay focused on the future and the goals ahead*
2) *Be a problem solver*
3) *Don't be afraid to ask for help*

Do not just go through tough times. Grow through them and get excited about achieving

something not just getting through something.
The things that you grow through make you who
you are. All things work for good if you can learn
to embrace all experiences that come your way.

- Tough times don't last.
- Tough people do.

Let bye-gones be bye-gones. If you keep a hard
heart then you only hurt yourself. Sometimes it
takes time to forgive but **'the immediate reward
of forgiveness is inner peace' (Dr Dwayne
Dyer).**

Your mind may not forget but you still need to
let go. You can't keep looking backwards. Focus
ahead on the future. Not forgiving only slows you
down because it gives you a heavy heart and
closes certain avenues, which could be the
gateway to you living your dreams. Let it go so
that you can really be free.

Muhammad Ali the world's greatest heavy weight boxer once said, 'Often it isn't the mountains ahead that wear you out, it is the little pebble in your shoe.'

Be an over comer and do not let obstacles slow you down or stop you. How can you appreciate light when there is no darkness? Nobody faces obstacles when they are going nowhere. Be strong and have courage. Do you have what it takes to pass the test? Where is your faith now?

How do you become a problem solver? Keep a positive mind; learn to be flexible along your journey to reaching your dreams. You are your biggest obstacle. Overcome the negatives in your mind and never ever give up.

YOU might as well...OVERCOME OBSTACLES...Let's do this!

Go the extra mile

If you are just surviving and struggling from day to day, understand that survival is not enough! It is time to go the extra mile. We all have something special to share with the world.

It is not important where we started from or where we are now. This should not determine where we finish. We can do more; we can become greater. Go for your dream(s), build your faith, fight for more of what you believe, face your fears, overcome your obstacles and lets go for more in life.

As you achieve things in life celebrate and congratulate yourself. You are living and

53

surviving. This is amazing. Be thankful and appreciate the good things that are going on in your life right now but do not get too comfortable. Do not become complacent. Aim higher! Go the extra mile.

This is how man made it into space. This is how we can now communicate via the internet using a mobile phone smaller than your hand. This is how Usain Bolt won Olympic Gold medals and has the world record for running 100m, 200m and the 4X100m relay. He could have just won the 100m Gold medal only but he decided that this was not enough, so he went for more.

Not only did he win three Gold medals and break three world records in the 2008 Beijing Summer Olympic games he wanted to repeat it and in the 2012 London Summer Olympic games, he was successful and repeated his victories'. However, this was not enough and he repeated his success in the Rio 2016 Olympic games. Between 2008 and 2016 he dreamed of repeating his success, trained hard, kept his faith, continued to stay disciplined, humble and pushed himself to overcome the challenges to help him go to the extra mile and become a champion again.

There is a difference between being ambitious and being greedy. Greed is about wanting something that you have not worked for or do not deserve. Being ambitious is all about having a strong desire and/or an eagerness to do more or become better.

Notice how many times you see successful sports people repeat their success. They often win trophy after trophy and championship after championship. For example, Sir Alex Ferguson the manager of Manchester United Football Club between 1986 and 2013 won 49 trophies as a manager and this included leading Manchester United to 13 Premier League titles, 5 FA Cups and 2 UEFA Champions League trophies. He was still hungry for more at the age of 70.

The Williams sisters in tennis are another example of two great leaders in their field who continue to strive for more even though as of 2015 they had won 13 doubles titles together and

over 110 singles women titles between them
which includes 28 grand slam women singles
titles. To top it off they also have eight Olympic
Gold medals between them.

Sir Alex Ferguson and the Williams sisters have
experienced many years of achieving some great
success. They have something inside of them
telling them to go the extra mile. You could say
that they are addicted to winning. Addicted to
success! They have a passion for what they are
doing and they are using their passion to help
them become part of history and have fulfilled
their dreams repeatedly.

Many people believe that wealthy people are greedy because they want more and more wealth. For many of them it is not more money they are chasing. They are chasing more success. They enjoy the challenge of going for more. They have a passion for overcoming challenges and their will to win is strong. They have BIG dreams and are prepared to fight for what they want and believe in.

Michael Jordan is one of the most famous sports personalities in the world. His inner ability to go the extra mile started early, as he actually never made his high school basketball team. However, by the end of his high school years he become one of the outstanding players and was selected as part of the McDonalds All-American Team and earned himself a basketball scholarship in the University of North Carolina.

Jordan helped lead his University basketball team to the national championship in 1982 and after three years at the University of North Carolina, he joined the Chicago Bulls in the NBA (National Basketball Association) in 1984.

Michael Jordan quickly emerged as a NBA star. He entertained the crowds with his highflying jumping ability, scoring ability and gained great respect for his amazing defense.

Jordan then retired in 1994 and decided to go and play professional baseball as he said that he had lost his desire to play the game after the murder of his father in July 1993. After a two word press conference ('I'm back'), he rejoined the Bulls in March 1995 and led them to three more consecutive NBA championships between 1996 and 1998.

Jordan retired for a second time in 1999, but later returned for two more NBA seasons between 2001 and 2003 as a member of the Washington Wizards. Even though Michael turned 40, during the 2003 season, he still managed to score 20 points or more in 50% of his games played.

Michael Jordan won three NBA championships retired, came back, won another three championships retired, then came back again, and broke some more records.

Michael Jordan is an example of someone who goes the extra mile even after achieving great success. He refuses to settle for what he has already achieved.

3 top tips to help you go the extra mile;

1) Know where you want to go because if you don't know where you are going, you will end up somewhere else
2) Break down the next mile into small steps
3) Keep learning and asking questions

Go the extra mile. Go for more in life and stay humble. Stay hungry for success and passionate about your goals and dreams.

- Press on
- Push harder
- Stretch your mind

- Use more of your skills and reach higher
- Do the best you can and then do a little bit more
- The sky is clearly no longer the limit because man has been going into space since 1961.

As humans, we are blessed to have the power of choice. Choose to reach your maximum potential.

A tree grows as tall as it possibly can, not just enough to blossom each year. Next time you get the chance, take time to notice how a plant leans and grows towards the light. That is the plants way of saying that they want more, they want to grow taller, and they want to grow greener leaves.
Just like sunlight, our inner strength and thoughts are given to us free but we need to make the choice to lean towards the light. Decide to let your light shine brighter.

> *Michael Jordan once said, 'Some people want it to happen, some wish it would happen, others make it happen.'*

It starts from the inside. Push on. Push through it all. You need to have enough fire on the inside to fight the problems on the outside. Go that extra in life!

Aim higher, make your goals bigger. Go for more in life. Reach for the stars. It is not over until the fat lady sings and you surpass your dreams. Believe that more is possible. More is achievable. Wanting more is ok. You are not being greedy you are being competitive; you are reaching for the stars because you want to replicate the star inside of you.

YOU might as well...GO THE EXTRA MILE...Let's do this!

Live with passion

Too many people end up living lives that they do not want. People end up in jobs that they do not like, communities that they forever moan about and do not want to live in. People that they smile at but wish they just went away.

Passion is all about having strong emotions and great enthusiasm. When you live with passion, you live life with a smile on the inside. Passion gives you energy. Living with passion will help you go further than your comfort zone. Living with passion will allow you to meet and inspire people you never thought you would meet. Living with passion will help you achieve more than you think you could with what you started with.

Attract the life that you desire by living with passion. Do the things you love. Do the things you enjoy. Do the things you are good at and are complimented on. Do the things that make you smile inside and out!

Living with passion brings more focus to your actions. Living with passion gives you more energy than other people who live passively. Living with passion allows you to keep going when you feel like giving up. It may even force you to do something that everyone else thinks is crazy but it makes sense to you. Do not worry, as it will make sense to everyone else later.

What would you do every day if you did not need to pay your bills? What would you wake up at 5am everyday for without the use of an alarm clock?

What do you spend your time doing and then say to yourself hours later, "WOW, is that the time already, time has flown by?" What makes you cry? What makes you sad or angry? What makes you excited, like a kid going to Disney World Florida in the morning? Your answers to these questions will help you identify some of your passions.

The first time I delivered finance training was an experience I will never forget. I was extremely nervous the weekend before. I could think of nothing else apart from the training session taking place on Monday afternoon. Half way through the training I remember saying to myself, "This is amazing". It was so much fun, time flew by and the group I was working with really appreciated the experience. This is now one of my life passions and one of my life goals is to become the greatest motivational finance trainer ever. Watch this space...

Passion is what helped make Muhammad Ali "The Greatest of All Time". Muhammad Ali first got into boxing when he was 12 years old. He was found fuming by a police officer in Louisville just after someone had stolen his bicycle. He told the police officer that he was going to "whoop" the person who took his bike. The police officer then told the young Muhammad Ali (known then as Cassius Clay) that he had better learn how to box first.

The young Muhammad Ali took on board this advice and 6 years later, he won the Light Heavyweight gold medal in the 1960 Summer Olympic Games in Rome.

Ali later went on to become the heavy weight champion of the world just a few years later. His fame grew not only because of his great boxing ability but also because of his character. He was well known for taunting his opponents before their encounters and he brought beauty and grace to the sport of boxing through his brilliant use of skill and character.

It is clear to see that Muhammad Ali started boxing with passion and maintained that passion. Even after a 4-year boxing ban because Ali refused to fight in the Vietnam War as it went against his values and principles. Muhammad Ali's passion for life outside of boxing inspired a generation including Dr Martin Luther King and helped take his status, respect and life achievements to a much higher level.

To maintain the high level of energy required to achieve your dreams and win fights that help you become the heavy weight champion of your world you need to live with passion. Energy is created in your mind first and passion is the fuel. Just as petrol fuels a car and allows it to move, the passion inside you is the fuel that takes you through the journey of life.

3 top tips to help you live with passion:

1) *Find and understand your passion(s)*
2) *Acknowledge that passion will help take you outside of your comfort zone*
3) *Use your passion to help you grow and inspire others*

Finding your passion is one of the success
secrets to life. True passions are found deep
within yourself. Sometimes when we discover our
passions, we run away from them, as they do not
fit in with our current lifestyle. Don't run away,
stay and fight. Find a way of including your newly
found passion in your daily lifestyle. Start small
and take it from there.

+ Passion is the difference between good and
  excellent
+ Passion is what takes human achievements
  to the next level
+ Passion helps you maintain loving
  relationships
+ Love with passion
+ Live and breathe with passion
+ Passionate actions and words inspire those
  around us
+ Passion helps us focus. Focus is very
  important as it helps us stay tuned in on
  the task ahead without being distracted.

**After you find your passion, the key is to
start trying to build your life around your**

passion. **Real passions are not time bound and last for a long time. They are deeper than material objects and things because material things such as cars, houses and money come and go.**

Have you ever had a conversation with someone where you asked them one question and they went on and on and on? They just did not stop talking. Their eyes lit up and their energy level increased the second that you mentioned the topic. That is an example of where someone has a passion.

- Live with more intensity
- Find a cause that is close to your heart and dedicate some of your time towards it
- Put a little more energy behind your actions
- Light the flame
- Get the fire burning inside of you
- Roar! Like a lion
- Can you feel the passion?
- ROAR again!

Living a passionate life often occurs after our heart has been touched by something. Use this energy and live with passion. The world is driven and led by strong passionate people. Good and bad. Even evil dictators have passion and high energy. The world needs your positive, good-hearted, passion.

Do the things you love. Try not to just chase money. Selling out is going against what you believe for commercial gain. Find your passion. Find out what you value. What would you do if you weren't paid for it? Then find a way to make money doing what you love.

YOU might as well...LIVE WITH PASSION...Let's do this!

Don't worry, be happy

To be happy you need to have a sense of achievement, inner peace and joy. This achievement could come from winning an award, passing a test, being a proud parent, sharing a special moment with a loved one, or even the feeling after you face and overcome a personal fear.

One secret to being happy is to be productive. Productiveness gives you confidence and a sense of achievement. Think about a time when you produced something, e.g. you baked a cake at school, painted a picture, made something out of wood or even strengthened a relationship. I am sure you felt a sense of happiness within, even if you didn't like the cake or thought that the picture didn't represent exactly what you had painted. The fact of knowing that you did something contributed to your happiness in that moment.

Happiness only lasts for a short period of time before our negative emotions start to kick in. We need to be everlasting and try to live a life that gives us eternal happiness. Find that special thing that gives you inner joy. Don't worry, be happy and smile because YOU are amazing!

You do not need a reason to be happy. I heard that when you smile it becomes infectious. Try it for yourself. Next time you are out n about smile at people and count how many of them smile back at you.

Smiling is contagious. Think about someone you know who is always smiling. I bet you smiled a little (either physically or internally) just thinking about them. Just think about the positive impact a simple smile can have.

Worry and anger are also contagious. Think about whom you know is always screwing their face, always angry, always worrying, complaining and negative. Take a second to reflect on the thoughts that went through your mind as that person came to mind. Did you feel your happiness increase or decrease?

Can you buy happiness? It has been said that money cannot buy happiness. This is partly true but it all depends on what you spend your money on. Try spending some money on someone else and see how it makes you feel. Notice also the difference in the feeling if you spend money on someone that you don't even know. It does not have to be something big, even a small gift that costs no money (such as a hug) can produce a lot of happiness for you. I dare you to try it and notice the difference in your level of happiness.

Many times, we look outside ourselves to try to find happiness. Sometimes you may find happiness from the outside world. However, remember that our control of the outer world is limited and temporary.

Brian Tracy another great motivational speaker has a quote that says, "You cannot control what happens to you but you can control your attitude towards what happens to you, and in that you will be mastering change rather than allowing it to master you".

Don't worry, be happy. There is no point worrying about things that we cannot control. Do not let worry take away your happiness because it just might not happen and even if it does happen, worry will not help make it better.

Lesley Calvin Brown is a top motivational speaker and speaker coach. He is also known as "Les Brown Mrs. Mamie Brown's baby boy". He and his twin brother were adopted by Mrs. Mamie Brown who was a single woman with very little education and money.

The story of Les Brown is quite amazing. He was put back in high school twice. He was referred to as "D .T." for "Dumb Twin". The label and stigma severely damaged his self-esteem for many years.

One of the main features of any Les Brown message that you hear is his charisma, high energy and happiness. Les Brown is always smiling, even in his younger days Les Brown was described as the class clown.

Les Brown always gets his audience smiling and laughing. Not only does he try to inspire them and pass on great wisdom and positive messages he also aims to get people to see beyond their current situation and to not worry about the future.

To find his true happiness Les Brown often shares the quote from Abraham Lincoln who said, "All that I am and all that I ever hope to be I owe to my mother". Les is always referencing his mother in all of his presentations and it is clear to see that his inner joy comes from striving for success and making his late mother proud.

I remember a joyful moment that came during a time when I had many worries on my mind. I was trying not to think about my worries and trying to focus on something positive. It was Christmas day and my nieces and nephews were sitting and hanging onto my brother's arms and legs as he sat on a chair in the kitchen. They were watching music videos on YouTube and they selected a music video from a group called Magic who had a song called Rude. I had never heard the song before but now I love it.

The joyful memory of my nieces and nephews all hanging onto my brother and singing the song together makes me smile every time I hear the song. It was a great moment and I used that to help me overcome my worry at the time as I decided to think of that moment anytime the negative thoughts crept in.

Happiness leads to joy and joy gives you strength. Genuine laughter is a sign of happiness for the moment and laughter helps maintain a healthy body. It takes more energy to frown than it does to smile. Why don't you give us a smile right now? ☺

3 top tips to help you pursue happiness;

1) Be thankful for everything good in our life
2) Take more time to appreciate the good things in your life
3) Take control of your thoughts and stop worrying

Many of us turn our back on happiness and choose to be miserable, unthankful and worriers.

+ Worry makes you devalue yourself and hate on others
+ Worry makes you imagine the worst
+ Worry takes away your dreams
+ Worry makes you over analyse a situation and jump to conclusions
+ Pick yourself up. Be happy
+ Rise above it!
+ Avoid the self destruction and negativity
+ Stay positive. Stay happy
+ Keep pushing on
+ Keep being productive

So what should you do instead of worry? Have faith! Share your concern(s) with friends and family, ask yourself questions, plan, prepare yourself and if you believe in the power of prayer, pray and have faith that everything works for the good.

One of my favorite poems written by Ralph Waldo Emerson starts by saying "Little minds have little worries. Big minds have no time for worries. As a cure for worry, work is better than whisky..."

Although smiling and laughing has been mentioned a lot in this chapter. Even if you do smile and laugh a lot, this does not necessarily mean that you are happy. Happiness is not always measured by a smile. You may seem happy on the outside but have to cry yourself to sleep each night!

"It isn't what you have, who you are, where you are, or what you are doing that makes you happy or unhappy. It is what you think about."

Money does not make everyone happy all of the time. Just think of all the unhappy rich people out there. The challenge is to be happy with yourself, then stay happy whilst making money.

Have you ever been around people who are happy and enthusiastic all the time even when you have been feeling miserable on the inside? That can be quite an annoying feeling. Let's find that same happiness and leave the misery behind. Sometimes we miss happiness by looking too far for things that are nearby. If you are still looking for a happy ending I suggest you start searching for a new beginning.

Here is a story to help us all think about what happiness is. There was a young boy in school. He was asked to write down what he wanted to be when he grew up. He wrote down three words! *'To be happy'.* His teacher then told him that he didn't understand the instructions.

The instructions were clear and were followed accurately. It seems that life has become unclear for many...life is a journey...find your happiness. Be grateful. Count your blessings. What makes you happy?

YOU might as well...DON'T WORRY, BE HAPPY...Let's do this!

Help others

When we were babies, which we all were, once upon a time. We relied 100% upon someone to help us survive. When we needed to eat someone was there to feed us. When we needed to be changed someone was there to change us. As we grow, our needs change but our cry for help often becomes quieter.

If you see someone crying on the inside offer your support and help them. Helping people is one of the best ways to put a smile on your face. Helping people helps you by making you happier by giving you a feeling of fulfillment.

Is the smaller man in the picture on the previous page falling or being helped up? Do you have a positive or negative mindset? Stay focused on the positives.

You will always get all you want in life, if you help enough people get what they want. Anne Frank, the young Jewish girl who had to hide from the Nazis during World War II, said in her famous diary, 'No one has ever become poor by giving'.

Think about a time when you gave some money to charity or helped an old person carry some bags up the stairs. Did it not help brighten up that moment of the day?

Sometimes we need to open our hearts before we can help others. By opening our hearts a little, we become more, sensitive and open minded towards those in need.

We need to love ourselves as well as loving others. When we have learnt to love ourselves, find happiness and confidence, it then becomes easier to be more loving to others around us including strangers. However, it is a catch 22, as often part of our happiness and confidence comes from helping and loving others so we might as well start spreading the love.

It can sometimes be difficult to help others due to personal situations so we do need to love and help ourselves at times. There is a saying that goes 'I want you to help yourself to help me'.

If we are not playing our part or pulling our weight then it becomes harder for the people around us that care about us. They will not want to see you fall down so they will reach out a help in hand and help you.

Some people are not so fortunate and do not have such a support network. This is why it is not just about helping our close friends and family.

Billy Graham a famous gospel preacher once said, 'God has given us two hands, one to receive with and the other to give with'.

Mary Jane Grant was born on 14 May 1805 in Jamaica. Her mother was a Jamaican nurse and healer and her father was a Scottish soldier. Mary last saw her father when she was 10 years old.

Mary loved to travel and visited Cuba, Britain and the Bahamas. Mary became Mrs. Seacole in 1836 when she married an English man called Edwin Seacole and they both ran a hotel together helping wounded soldiers. In 1844 Edwin died, Mary became a widow and soon after the hotel that she ran burnt down.

In 1854, Mary heard about the Crimea war in Russia. She was confident that her knowledge of tropical medicine could be useful, and after hearing of the poor medical provisions for wounded soldiers, she travelled to London to volunteer as a nurse. When Mary arrived in Britain, she tried to work in a team of nurses led by Florence Nightingale.

Mary was told that no more nurses were needed. Mary was not put off by this so she decided to raise some money with her friend Thomas Day and travelled to the war by ship. When she arrived, the battles were fierce and many soldiers were cold, hungry and wounded. During this time, the government did not really take care of the soldiers so they had to take care of themselves.

Mary and her friend Thomas set up a hotel made out of metal sheets and helped serve the soldiers hot food and drinks. Mary also sold warm clothes, blankets, boots and saddles for horses. She nursed the sick and wounded men and helped them fight off diseases such as Cholera. Mary's work was much appreciated by the soldiers and they started calling her Mother Seacole.

Mary used horses to travel close to the fighting. She saw cannon balls being fired and lots of fighting. She was fearless and her passion for helping people outweighed all of her fears. In 1856, the war ended. Mary returned to the UK with very little money and many of the soldiers wrote letters to Mary and the local newspaper to thank her and tell what a wonderful help she had been.

Mary Seacole died in 1881, aged 76 and buried in London. In her will, she requested that a home for dead soldiers' children be built. Even in her passing, she wanted to help people.

It is quite amazing to see the passion and sacrifices that Mary was prepared to go through to help people using her nursing skills and knowledge. Mary Seacole did things few other women of her time did. She made her own way in the world and helped everyone that she met by mixing medicine with kindness.

Helping others can bring great pleasure to two people's lives, one of them being yours.

> 3 top tips to help people;
>
> 1) Open your heart a little more
> 2) Take time out of your busy schedule
> 3) Use your skills to help others who
>   don't have the same skills

When we open our hearts, a little more we will hear pain and sadness in people's words without the words pain and sadness being mentioned. The injustice and unfairness that is happening around us will become clearer to see. As our heart opens, we feel closer to people without having to touch them with our hands.

Helping others is not just about giving money. Sometimes a simple word of encouragement, a smile or even a little bit of time can go a very long way.

Be genuine, smile for real at people, and give compliments when they are due. Encourage people when they are both up and down. If someone has done a good job, it costs you nothing to say 'well done'.

Humans do not just need food to survive; we also need words of encouragement and love.

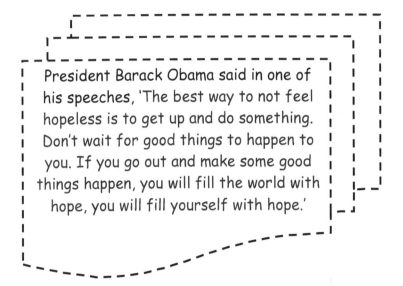

President Barack Obama said in one of his speeches, 'The best way to not feel hopeless is to get up and do something. Don't wait for good things to happen to you. If you go out and make some good things happen, you will fill the world with hope, you will fill yourself with hope.'

You have skills and knowledge that others don't have. Help people where you can. You can help others whilst going for your dreams. You may even realize your true passion whilst helping others.

YOU might as well...HELP OTHERS...Let's do this!

Learn a little

Learning is not just about going to school, college and then going on to University. In other words academic education. There are several different types of education in addition to academic education such as financial, business, professional, and spiritual education to name a few. All of these are critical to helping you achieve your dreams.

Learning keeps you alive for longer because it helps stimulate your brain. If your brain is working, you can smile because it means that you are still living. If you are not learning, it means that you are not growing and if you are not growing then you can't expect to receive or achieve more from life.

Learning helps you overcome obstacles and prepares you better for the battles of life. Learning helps, you build your confidence and understanding. Most importantly, learning empowers you to do the things that you want to do. It helps you make better-informed decisions for the future.

There is a saying that goes; 'most people don't know and they think they know but they don't know that they don't know'. I believe this saying comes from the African proverb, 'He who knows not, that he knows not is a compound fool'.

Learn a little whilst you can. Be smart about what you learn. Be smart about how you learn and whom you learn from. If you think education is expensive then you should try ignorance. Overcoming ignorance will help you save time, money, energy and increase your

chances of succeeding in whatever it is you want to do.

Learn through life's experiences. Insanity is said to be doing the same thing over and over again but expecting a different result. It is very likely that there is someone who has done what you want to do already so reach out and ask them for help. If you cannot speak to them physically then use the internet to connect and learn about them.

One of the largest resources that our generation does not take full advantage of is the elderly around us. Just think of the amount of knowledge older people have picked up over the years. When you get the opportunity to speak with the elderly take full advantage as they have survived years of obstacles, achieved a lot of success and have lots of potential to help us achieve our dreams and avoid painful experiences.

Learning is very necessary if you want to have more. It is also necessary that you become more to stay happy.

The only thing constant in the world is change and if we do not constantly aim to improve ourselves by learning then we will be left behind. We are now in the information age where money, success and value are all generated by having and using the right information at the right time.

Eric Thomas says that; 'Information changes situations'. What is your current situation? If you want to find yourself in a new situation then you need some new information.

Know everything and know nothing simultaneously.

Booker Taliaferro was born into a life of slavery in Franklin County, Virginia, USA. He never knew his real father and as his mother Jane was a slave working as a cook he had no choice but to live an early life of slavery.

Booker started working on a farm estate from an early age and this was where he was exposed to formal education. There was a schoolhouse near

91

the farm and Booker saw young children that looked like they were the same age as him sitting down at desks and reading books. He immediately felt drawn to this and wanted to also learn at school but at this time, it was illegal to teach slaves to read and write.

The great news came when the American Civil War ended in 1865 and an announcement was made that all slaves (most of who were in the southern part of the country) were to be set free. This allowed Booker and his mother to move to Malden, West Virginia, USA. It was here that Booker's mother married Washington Ferguson, who became Booker's stepfather. Booker took his stepfather's first name as his surname so he became Booker T Washington.

Booker T Washington worked in a salt mine with his stepfather to help the family, as they were very poor. Booker's mother did manage to buy Booker a book, which is how he learnt to read and write through self-study.

Booker soon got a job as a houseboy. The lady of the house took a liking to Booker and noticed his intelligence and admired his honesty and desire to get an education so she allowed him to go to school for one hour every day during the winter months.

Booker T. Washington left home in 1872 and walked 500 miles to Hampton. He went to the Normal Agricultural Institute and he convinced the administrators to let him attend the school whilst he took a job as a janitor to help pay for his tuition. Again due to his passion for education and hard work he was offered a scholarship.

Booker was later offered a job as a teacher at Hampton after he graduated. In 1881, an approved budget was given to Booker T Washington's mentor General Armstrong to fund a school teaching freed slaves. Booker was recommended for this role and the Tuskegee Normal and Industrial Institute (now known as Tuskegee University) was born.

He remained the principal of the Tuskegee Normal and Industrial Institute until his death in 1915.

Booker T Washington had a passion and eagerness to learn so much that it took him from a life of slavery to being an advisor to the White House where he was often asked to advise on racial issues and education.

I have travelled to many under developed countries in four of the world's continents and the most common ambition I hear from young people or their parents is to be able to receive or provide their children with a good education.

There are approximately 1 billion people around the world today who cannot read this book because they are unable to read. Be thankful that you had the opportunity to take your learning this far and you can read this book. Think of how empowering being able to read has been in your life so far.

Ever since I read my first book at the age of 21 whilst recovering from TB, I have been a student of success. I call myself a lifelong learner. In addition to academic studies, I have taken the opportunity to learn professional skills in finance and accountancy as well as personal skills such as leadership, teamwork, relationships and communication. These are known as soft skills but I call them essential life skills.

Everyone needs money and I definitely recommend that everyone build his or her knowledge and understanding in the area of money (financial education). Jim Rohn a great modern day philosopher said, 'Formal education will make you a living; self education will make you a fortune.'

Studying the word of God and different religions has also been of great value in my life. This helped me have a clearer understanding for the spiritual direction in my life.

What if there is some more information out there that could empower you just as much as being able to read has done for your life? You might as well learn a little.

3 top tips to help you learn more?

1) Learn from history including our past experiences
2) Learn from our elders and mentors (they have been there, done that and got the t-shirt to prove it!)
3) Learn through reading and researching

Learning can also be done through our experiences. This is a slow way of learning and depending on how honest we are with ourselves; this method may take a very long time. It is ok to make mistakes. Everyone makes mistakes but making the same mistake more than once is a sign that you did not learn from your first mistake.

Nelson Mandela said, 'Education is the most powerful weapon which you can use to change the world.'

Maya Angelou said, 'I did then what I knew how to do. Now that I know better, I do better."

Using knowledge can turn your life around. Those who think they know really don't. Aim to be a life-long learner. It is said that we only know something when we are living it. People die every day because of a lack of knowledge.

There are many different ways to learn but the main two are through mentorship and pain. Used knowledge is the key to overcoming obstacles, our fears and achieving our dreams.

YOU might as well...LEARN A LITTLE...Let's do this!

Leave a legacy

When you see the word legacy, what is the first thing that comes to mind? A will, money, a family estate? I like to think of a legacy as something bigger than material things. I think a true legacy is something bigger than money and a mansion. I believe that a true legacy is a footprint left on Earth that continues to help your friends, family and your community after you are gone.

Some people manage to leave some simple legacies like words of wisdom or even a family recipe that continues to bring joy to the family through food and unity. Some people leave a legacy in their local community such as the impact of a successful community project that has helped many people. Some people go further afield and leave a legacy in the world. A dream like Dr Martin Luther King Jr (see chapter 1), a university like Booker T Washington or even some outstanding sporting achievements like Michael Jordan (see chapter 6).

The past or the future, which one creates your picture? Are you living for now or are you thinking about the future that you want to live and the impact that you want to have during your time on Earth. The honest answer to this question is shown through your actions.

'Do not go where the path may lead. Instead create a new path and leave a trail.' Ralph Waldo Emerson.

Let's play a quick game. Name or sing a Bob Marley song to yourself right now in your head or aloud. I guarantee that at least 90% of people who read this book will be able to name or sing a Bob Marley song.

Robert Nesta Marley better known as Bob Marley was born on 6 February 1945 on the Caribbean island of Jamaica in a rural mountain village called Nine Miles. His mother Cedella Marley was a young woman when she had Bob and his father last saw Bob Marley when he was 5 years old.

When Bob was a young boy, he moved to the capital of Jamaica, Kingston with his mother as she was looking for a better life for her and her son. In Kingston, Bob and his mother settled in Trench Town, which at this time was well known for crime and poverty.

Bob left school at the age of 14 and spent some time being an apprentice welder but his passion for music was really his true love so he decided to focus on that. Bob attended vocal classes held in the local community of Trench Town by a local resident and singer by the name of Joe Higgs.

It was at these community classes that he was introduced to Peter Tosh. Peter, Bob and Bob's childhood friend Bunny formed the legendary vocal group The Wailers. It was not all great at the start and the group had to overcome many obstacles such as additional members joining and leaving, finding a record deal, selling their singles and receiving no financial rewards all whilst trying to survive in the Trench Town ghetto.

Bob married his first wife Rita Marley in 1966 and moved to the USA for a few months with his mother where he briefly worked in a factory. It was during this time that Bob and his wife Rita turned to the Rastafarian way of life and begun to grow dreadlocks. Bob soon returned to Jamaica and joined up with the other Wailer's and included his wife Rita as a female vocalist. They set up a record shop in Trench Town but this was still not enough to take their music to places beyond Trench Town and Kingston Jamaica.

After a few years of trying and still producing great music, The Wailers were in London and managed to get a deal with Island records. This led the Wailers to receive some international media and the opportunity to tour England and the USA. After a couple of years of success Bob's two friends Bunny and Peter Tosh decided to leave the group so the group became Bob Marley and The Wailers.

The new group recorded another album and went on another very successful European tour. By 1976, Bob Marley was a global reggae star. With Bob's success came some hatred and in December of 1976 two days before Bob was going to perform in a free 'Smile Jamaica' concert an assignation attempt was made. Luckily, Bob escaped with minor injuries. His wife Rita had to have surgery to remove a bullet that grazed her head but Bob's manager Don Taylor was shot five times and crucially wounded.

This did not stop Bob from performing at the 'Smile concert'. After performing at the concert, Bob flew to London where he stayed for the next

18 months. Bob returned to Jamaica and performed at the 'One Love Peace' concert in April 1978. It was during this time that the political war had led to a surge in gang wars in Jamaica. During the performance, Bob Marley got the Jamaica Labor Party (JLP) leader Edward Seaga and Prime Minister Michael Manley of the People's National Party (PNP) onstage and asked them to shake hands.

Bob Marley made his first trip to Africa at the end of 1978 visiting Kenya and Ethiopia. Bob Marley made a big mark on Africa and especially Zimbabwe where he was invited to perform at the official Independence Ceremony after his song 'Zimbabwe' had become the anthem that helped the people of Zimbabwe through the last of their struggle for liberation and Independence.

Bob Marley and The Wailers went on their final tour of Europe and the USA in 1980 where they performed to record breaking crowds. It was in Pittsburgh that Bob Marley performed for the

last time in public in September 1980. Bob
Marley died eight months later in May 1981.

However, the legend and legacy of Bob Marley
did not die in May 1981. Bob Marley's music and
his messages continue to help people through the
obstacles of life today. His music is still used to
celebrate the fight for freedom, inequality,
peace and revolution.

When you look, back and read about famous
people including Bob Marley (as above), very
rarely are you told how much money they made.
What we do know and read about them is the
impact they made during their time on Earth. For
example, what do you think of when Dr Martin
Luther King comes to mind? How about Oprah
Winfrey? Fella Kuti? Nina Simone? Or Nelson
Mandela? I am sure a number with a pound or
dollar sign in front of the number did not come
to mind first!

It is the passion, love, achievements, struggles,
impact on the community and fights they have
faced and overcome that we hear and think

about. These are the important things in life. These are the lasting legacies that we leave behind!

Leaving a legacy is no easy thing. It takes a dedicated life to leave a footprint on Earth.

3 top tips to help you leave a legacy?

1) *Stay focused on your journey, mission and dreams*
2) *Be dedicated to your values and principles and fight for the causes that touch your heart*
3) *Help inspire the next generation*

Be a role model for our kids, be a mentor and be an example for young people to look up to. **Who do you think is the best person to walk the Earth in the modern world? Why not become that person for someone else.**

My legacy is that I stayed on course...
from the beginning to the end, because I
believed in something inside of me.

Tina Turner

Live the life you deserve, take responsibility for your life, embrace the responsibility of leadership. Believe that God has preserved you for higher things. Look for the signals and ignore the cost that it is going to take to climb the mountain. At the end of your life, what would you want to have traded your time on Earth for?

How you will be remembered? What do you plan to leave the world as your inheritance? Always think about making a bigger impact. Have a goal that leaves a legacy for at least 100 years after you are gone.

YOU might as well...LEAVE A LEGACY...Let's do this!

Pass it on

Teach. Take the time to teach someone a skill you know. This could be teaching your grandma how to email, teaching your child to ride a bike, teaching your colleague a short cut on a computer programme.

There is a proverb in Africa that says 'when you take the elevator to go up, you must always remember to send it back down'.

Jim Rohn said, "Study, practice, teach". Think about your best life and schoolteachers. What did they pass on to you? Focus on the positives and pass that on. I have been blessed to have experienced some great teachers along the way.

One of my life teachers taught me to be
excellent in the challenge in front of me.

My Primary school teacher Mr. Spruth helped
ignite my passion for working with numbers. He
helped me master my times tables at the age of
nine. My math's teacher in secondary school took
my skills to a completely new level. Mr. Matti also
had a saying that I still use today. He would
always say that there are many ways to skin a
cat. I always tell myself this when it comes to
living life or solving a problem. There is always
more than one answer.

Once you have acquired knowledge, turn it into
wisdom by applying your knowledge to your life
and then pass it on.

Tell me and I will forget. Get me to write it down
and I might lose the piece of paper. Involve me
and I will be empowered and remember for a
lifetime.

Life change starts with inspiration and
motivation to learn something new and as we

study or practice this new thing, we get the confidence to take action. When we take action and we can see that our life is turning around we get excited and want to share it with someone.

Be a leader, a trendsetter and pass it on.

Pass it on for the future..., which we call life.

Did you notice anything about all the icons mentioned during the chapters that you have just read and hopefully been inspired from?

I could have used any one of the icons for any of the chapters. Looking into the lives of these historic leaders in more detail teaches us how Dr Martin Luther King teamed up and worked with Rosa Parks and Maya Angelou. Mohamed Ali

YOU might as well...

helped inspire MLK to openly oppose the Vietnam war.

Mary Seacole's passion for helping others took her to the front line of a war and extreme weather conditions. Even after experiencing many setbacks in her life she went the extra mile and continued to help others and left a legacy helping children.

All of the icons I have mentioned in the book had to overcome several obstacles. They used the pain from the obstacle and turned it into positives.

Maya Angelou's big break came when she wrote about her life experiences in 'I Know Why the Caged Bird Sings'. Michael Jordan failed to get into his high school basketball team but became obsessed with winning. To be a winner you have to dig deep within to overcome obstacles as well as learn all you need to be a master of your craft. Bob Marley's passion for music is evident in all of his songs and his fight for his beliefs continues today through his music.

Eric Thomas not only turned his life around with a new set of values and principles, he learned a lot too. He used his knowledge to transform his life and passed on his wisdom. Some of which I received, used and passed on to you.

Think about the struggles that Les Brown had to overcome to become happy. He wrote a book titled 'Live your dreams'. This was after he had achieved many of his dreams. The challenges facing Booker T Washington were big. Can you imagine yourself walking 500 miles to get the opportunity to learn with no guarantee it will work out?

All the icons had to overcome obstacles and went the extra mile even after achieving some success. They all achieved more than their dreams and left a legacy, which continues to inspire us today.

Many of the icons mentioned in this book started with very humble beginnings and they made it happen. If they can do it, we can do it.

Build your faith. Be positive always. Mark Twain the writer said, 'The secret of getting ahead is getting started'. What is your dream? What do you need to learn to help you win? Find a way to do more for others than anyone else.

Get started. Use this book to help you move towards your dream. What are you passionate about? We are all motivators, unique and special...lets continue to all motivate each other... you might as well!

Make a choice. The power of choice and decision-making is amazing. Remember that you are special. You are unique and you are amazing.

YOU might as well...PASS IT ON...Let's do this!

Conclusion

Ending this book, I want to **challenge** you. Go get a pen and some paper and write down your answer to the 12 questions below.

1) Describe what you want all of your close relationships, health, career, business and wealth to look like in 10 years.
2) How can you increase your understanding and relationship with God?
3) What are your top ten life values?
4) If you could overcome one fear forever, which one would it be?
5) What is slowing you down?
6) Do you know when you stop trying? What do you need to do to get yourself to try harder?
7) What gets you excited or angry? Think about why.
8) What is the first thing that comes to mind (after you say I don't know), when I ask; what makes you happy? What do you need to think of to make yourself smile inside?

9) Who would you love to be able to help the most in your family, your friends and your community? Where do they need your help?

10) What do you need to learn more about in your relationships, health, career, business and wealth?

11) When you die, how would you like people to remember you?

12) Who will you pass this book onto?

Well done for finding the energy and taking the time to answer the questions. Now use the three top tips in each chapter to make a plan of action for each question.

You are now well on your way. Keep going. Keep believing. Stay blessed, stay amazing.

Segun

About the author

Segun is a Management Accountant and a Motivational Finance Trainer who has a passion for working with numbers and people. He is a lifelong learner and a believer in the hope of the world.

Segun was born in Hackney, London and raised in a small town in Cambridgeshire for the first 10 years of his life before returning to Hackney and the fast life of the city. From a young age, Segun realized that the world was not a fair place as he observed the difference in lifestyles of people. This made him ask many questions that he is still finding answers to today.

Life has not always been easy for Segun and from a young age he suffered with rage and anger which continued into his teenage years where he started to rebel against life and walk down a negative path. The best year of his life came when he almost died from TB, which made him home bound for 6 months. It was this that helped Segun read his first book at the age of 21 and that opened his mind to a completely new understanding of the world and life.

There have been many things that have and continue to help Segun focus on the positive and possibilities of life. These include his faith in God, his family, mentors, the vision for his life and his commitment to learning.

His story continues ... the best motivational finance trainer, a great husband, a dedicated father, the best brother, a good son and an eternal life ambassador...

Connect with Segun Olowookere via LinkedIn or email: slowooke@gmail.com

#0182 - 051216 - C0 - 210/148/6 - PB - DID1677642